ALI

THE GREATEST

TRIVIA, FACTS AND QUOTES

NEW
HOLLAND

CONTENTS

Introduction

Muhammad Ali (1942–2016)

The life of Muhammad Ali—born Cassius Marcellus Clay in Louisville, Kentucky, in 1942—was one full of contradictions. Born of humble origins to a poor black family in the segregated 'Deep South' of America, Ali rose to become the greatest sportsperson of the 20th century and to be loved and admired around the world.

Poorly educated, Ali was one of the smartest self-promoters in the history of professional sport. Nobody had ever heard anyone—especially a black kid from Kentucky—talk the way he did, especially about himself. Baptized a Christian at the age of 12, within a decade he would change his religion and his name and become a spokesman and preacher of one of the most militant sects in America—the Nation of Islam.

Starting his professional boxing career as an

underdog, he became the greatest boxer in history. The sport gave him the opportunity to travel the world, win an Olympic gold medal and eventually capture the world heavyweight championship. It also provided him with the chance to educate himself as he travelled the world, especially in Africa and the Middle East, and to mix with ordinary people from many different walks of life.

At his very heart, Muhammad Ali was a pacifist and civil rights activist and, in the context of the 1960s, maybe even the 'Martin Luther King' of the ring. For a man who made his living fighting opponents in the boxing ring, in honoring his religious beliefs Ali readily declined military service in the Vietnam War that would have seen him fight other ethnic minorities in a faraway land.

The result of Ali's stance was to have his livelihood taken away from him. For three years, from the age of 25 to 28—an athlete's peak years in most sports—Ali was denied a boxing license as he appealed his conviction for avoiding the draft. When he came back to the ring in 1970, he had to prove himself to the world all over again and again!

Ali became the first fighter to win the heavyweight championship three times. But after announcing his retirement in 1979, against his and even our better judgment, he tempted fate and made not one, but two, comebacks in 1980 and 1981, failing both times. The losses made him more human, but he would pay a high price for his continued exposure to head trauma. When Parkinson's disease took hold of him in the

1980s, it was a cruel blow to a boxer who had prided himself on his good looks and athleticism.

Ali made many mistakes in his life: the failed marriages, the affairs, the comebacks, and the loss of millions of dollars as his increasing entourage and even members of his own family bled him dry. Ali could also be bigoted, even racist, in his own way when he readily espoused the militant views of his faith which called for the segregation of the races and the destruction of white society.

But like all good people of faith, Ali grew as a person and was able to reconcile what he believed with how he could make a difference in the real world. In his final years, no longer able to communicate freely or move easily, he devoted his strength and attention to charitable causes and the promotion of peace around the world.

It was said of his incredible life that Ali was able to shake off all the negative aspects of his personality and beliefs as Parkinson's disease ravaged his body. In his final years, Ali humbly radiated both light and love. When he lit the cauldron at the 1996 Atlanta Olympics, Ali lit something inside us all as well.

Of all the biographies and articles written about Ali during the past five decades, can a little book of sports records, quotable quotes and pop culture trivia possibly shed any light on the true nature of the man? Perhaps not, but I challenge you to read these pages and not shake your head in wonder at a truly amazing career; to remember what the man stood for or merely raise a smile.

Ali, the eternal prankster, would love that.

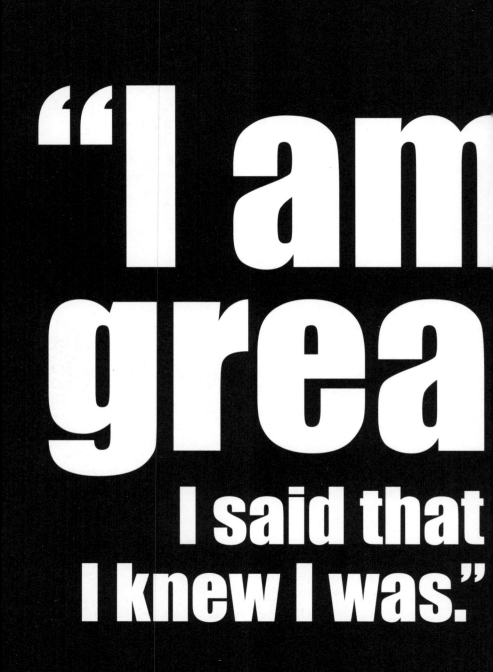

"I am grea

I said that
I knew I was."

the

test.

even before

Muhammad Ali's Family

Father:
Cassius Clay Sr. (1912–1990)

Mother:
Odessa Grady Clay (1917–1994)

Brother:
Rahman Ali (born Rudolph Valentino Clay, 1943–   )

★ ★ ★ ★

DID YOU KNOW?

Rahman Ali is the younger brother of Muhammad Ali and a former heavyweight boxer. While Rahman would inevitably be in the shadows of his older brother, he did achieve success in his professional boxing career, winning 14 of his 18 professional bouts. Like his older brother, Rahman also converted to the Nation of Islam and is believed to have been the one who influenced Ali in his conversion. Both brothers changed their names upon converting to Islam.

The Nation of Islam is an African-American movement that was founded in Detroit, United States in 1930 to improve the spiritual, social and economic welfare of African Americans in the United States, and all of humanity.

★ ★ ★ ★

Muhammad Ali was born Cassius Marcellus Clay in Louisville, Kentucky to parents Cassius Marcellus Clay Sr. and Odessa Grady Clay, the oldest of their two sons. His father was a painter by trade, painting billboards and signs. He also boasted an array of artistic talents, including music and dancing. Ali once championed his father as "the fanciest dancer in Louisville". Perhaps this is where the future boxing great inherited his famous moves.

Ali's mother, Odessa Clay, worked as a domestic when raising her two sons. She is noted as being a prime figure of influence in Ali's life, and was supportive of his early boxing ventures. From Ali's early days training at the local gym to his professional fights, Ali's mother was often present ring-side and shared in his dreams for boxing greatness.

"My principles are more important than the money or my title."

Cassius Clay, Amateur Fight Record

1954–1959 Clay won six Kentucky Golden Gloves championships, two national Golden Gloves titles, and two AAU (Amateur Athletic Union) crowns.

★ ★ ★ ★

DID YOU KNOW?

At the age of 12, the young Clay knocked on neighbors' doors in Louisville to tell them about his upcoming amateur fights which were often shown on a local TV station. This was the genesis of the future champion's ability to shamelessly self-promote his fights.

★ ★ ★ ★

After having his bicycle stolen, 12-year-old Cassius Clay reported the theft to Louisville police officer Joe Martin. True to his fighting spirit, Clay vowed to seek revenge on the culprit and to "whup whoever stole it". These words prompted officer Martin, who also worked as a boxing trainer, to introduce Clay to the world of boxing and fellow trainer Fred Stoner. Within six weeks of training, Clay made his amateur boxing debut which he won in a split-decision. Over the following years, Clay went on to win six Kentucky Golden Gloves titles, two National Golden Gloves titles (1959 and 1960) and two National Amateur Athletic Union titles (1956 and 1959). By the age of 18, Clay had become a proven fighter, with an amateur record of 100 wins to only eight losses.

"The fact is, I was never too bright in school. I ain't ashamed of it, though ... I said I was 'The Greatest', I never said I was the smartest!"

1960 Rome Olympics
Light Heavyweight Division (81kg)

 R1.   Bye

 R2.   Cassius Clay (USA) def. Yvon Becaus (BEL),
stoppage—2nd round

 QF.   Cassius Clay (USA) def. Gennadiy Shatkov (URS),
5–0

 SF.   Cassius Clay (USA) def. Anthony Madigan (AUS),
5–0

 F.   Cassius Clay (USA) def. Zbigniew Pietrzykowski
(POL), 5–0

"To make America the greatest is my goal, So I beat the Russians, and I beat the Pole, and for the USA won the medal of gold."

DID YOU KNOW?

Upon returning back to his hometown Louisville following his Olympic win, Clay was faced with much racism, including being denied service at a number of "whites-only" restaurants. Fuelled with anger after one such incident, Clay threw his Olympic gold medal into the Ohio River. Desipte Clay's decision to throw away his Olympic medal, he initially had cherished it, wearing it for two days straight, even when he went to bed.

It was not until June 2014, 54 years after an enraged Clay hurled his gold medal into the river, that the medal was allegedly retrieved from the muddy banks.

★ ★ ★ ★

1960 Rome Olympics

Clay burst onto the international boxing scene during the 1960 Rome Olympics, defeating experienced Polish opponent Zbigniew Pietrzykowski to snatch the light-heavyweight gold medal. Clay's overwhelming fear of flying almost stood between the boxer and his 1960 Olympic victory. Just weeks prior, Clay attempted to withdraw from the Olympic Games, but it was trainer Joe Martin who convinced the nervous flyer to compete.

Ali was soon hailed an American hero, but this did not make him immune to the scourge of racism in the US at the time.

★ ★ ★ ★

DID YOU KNOW?

Despite being only 18, Cassius Clay defeated three-time European champion Zbigniew Pietrzykowski to win the gold medal. Following his victory in Rome in the light-heavyweight division, Clay was visited by World Heavyweight Champion Floyd Patterson. "Look after that heavyweight title," the brash teenager told the quietly spoken Patterson. "Keep it warm for me in the next two years when I will be ready to take it off you."

★ ★ ★ ★

"Now I had won the gold medal. But it didn't mean anything, because I didn't have the right color skin."

"Boxing is a lot of white men watching two black men beat each other up."

At 18 years of age, shortly following his Olympic win, Cassius Clay embarked on his professional career and signed with the Louisville Sponsoring Group. The consortium of rich, white Kentucky businessmen agreed upon a payment of $10,000 cash, and $4,000 a year over a two-year period—the equivalent of almost $145,000 altogether in today's currency.

Clay began his career with a win against Tunney Hunsaker, overwhelming his opponent in six rounds with his speed, strength and agile footwork. Clay worked hard to overcome the flaws in his early boxing style including hanging his hands too low which left his head exposed and rearing his head backwards in defense. Throughout his career, it was his split-second reaction time and leg speed that gave him his advantage over his opponents.

Muhammad Ali (aka Cassius Clay) Professional Fight Record

M1. v Tunney Hunsaker (US)
Louisville, KY (United States), October 29, 1960
UD 6 (6) Win: 1–0 Record (18 years, 286 days)

M2. v Herb Siler (US)
Miami Beach, FL (United States), December 27, 1960
KO 4 (8) Win: 2–0 Record (18 years, 345 days)

M3. v Tony Esperti (US)
Miami Beach, FL (United States), January 17, 1961
TKO 3 (8), Win: 3–0 Record (19 years, 0 days)

M4. v Jim Robinson (US)
Miami Beach, FL (United States), February 7, 1961
KO 1 (8), Win: 4–0 Record (19 years, 21 days)

M5. v Donnie Fleeman (US)
Miami Beach, FL (United States), February 21, 1961
TKO 7 (8) Win: 5–0 Record (19 years, 35 days)

"Defense ain't the hands, it's the legs."

M6. v LaMar Clark (US)
Louisville, KY (United States) April 9, 1961
KO 2 (10), Win: 6–0 Record (19 years, 92 days)

M7. v Duke Sabedong (US)
Las Vegas, NV (United States) June 26, 1961
UD 10 (10) Win: 7–0 Record (19 years, 160 days)

M8. v Alonzo Johnson (US)
Louisville, KY (United States) July 22, 1961
UD (10) Win: 8–0 Record (19 years, 186 days)

M9. v Alex Miteff (Argentina)
Louisville, KY (United States) October 7, 1961
TKO 6 (10), Win: 9–0 Record (19 years, 263 days).

M10. v Willi Besmanoff (W.Germany)
Louisville, KY (United States) November 29, 1961
TKO 7 (10), Win: 10–0 Record (19 years, 316 days)

M11. v Sonny Banks (US)
New York, NY (United States) February 10, 1962
TKO 4 (10), Win: 11–0 Record (20 years, 24 days)

M12. v Don Warner (US)
Miami Beach, FL (United States) March 28, 1962
TKO 4 (10), Win: 12–0 Record (20 years, 70 days)

M13. v George Logan (US)
New York, NY (United States) April 23, 1962
TKO 4 (10), Win: 13–0 Record (20 years, 96 days)

M14. v Billy Daniels (US)
New York, NY (United States) May 19, 1962
TKO 7 (10), Win: 14–0 Record (20 years, 122 days)

Within his first two years as a professional boxer, Clay continued his winning streak against a score of seasoned opponents including Tony Esperti, Jim Robinson, Donnie Fleeman, LaMar Clark, Alonzo Johnson and Willi Besmanoff. By the end of 1961 he had an impressive 10–0 fight record and was starting to garner national media attention.

In 1962, Floyd Patterson was defeated by Sonny Liston for the World Heavyweight Championship. When 21-year-old Cassius Clay was asked who he considered to be the best boxer in the world, his reply was honest and straight to the point: "Cassius Clay".

"I'm so fast that last night I turned off the light switch in my hotel room and got into bed before the room was dark."

NO HOME TV

12 Rds. HEAVYWEIGHT TITLE
ELIMINATION BOUT 12 Rds.

LOS ANGELES SPORTS ARENA

THUR. NOV. 15 7:30 P.M.

ARCHIE   CASSIUS
MOORE VS CLAY

World's Light Heavyweight Champion   The Undefeated Louisville Lip

ALL SEATS RESERVED
Tax Included
RINGSIDE $25
MAIN FLOOR RES. $15
LOGES $25 & $15
BALCONY $10 & $7.50

AN OLYMPIC BOXING
CLUB PROMOTION
Phone RI 9-5171

TICKETS ON SALE HERE

COLBY POSTER PRINTING CO. 1332 W. 12th Place, Los Angeles 15

M15. v Alejandro Lavorante (ARG)
Los Angeles, CA (United States) July 20, 1962
KO 5 (10), Win: 15–0 Record (20 years, 184 days)

M16. v Archie Moore (US)
Los Angeles, CA (United States) November 15, 1962
TKO 4 (10), Win: 16–0 Record (20 years, 302 days)

M17. v Charlie Powell (US)
Pittsburgh, PA (United States) January 24, 1963
KO 3 (10), Win: 17–0 Record (21 years, 7 days)

M18. v Doug Jones (US)
New York, NY (United States) March 13, 1963
UD 10 (10), Win: 18–0 Record (21 years, 55 days)

M19. v Henry Cooper (UK)
London, (United Kingdom) June 18, 1963
TKO 5 (10), Win: 19–0 Record (21 years, 152 days)

"Archie's been living off the fat of the land. I'm here to give him his pension plan. When you come to the fight don't block the door. 'Cause you'll all go home after round four."

EMPIRE STADI
WEMBLEY

JACK SOLOMON

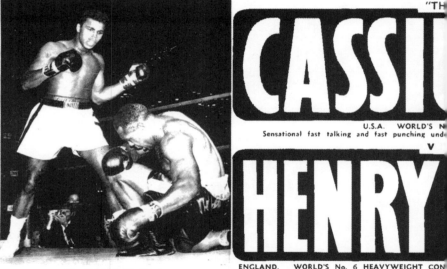

DOORS
OPEN
5.30

TH E WORLD'S GREATEST SHOWM
"THE LOUISVILLE LIP"

ELIMINATING CONTEST FOR THE HEA
10 x 3 MI
"TH

CASSI

U.S.A.   WORLD'S N
Sensational fast talking and fast punching unde

v

HENRY

Clay K.O.'s Archie Moore

ENGLAND.   WORLD'S No. 6 HEAVYWEIGHT CON

I'M T
I'M T

SAYS CASSIUS MARCIUS CLAY:

WATCH PRESS AND POSTERS FOR SENSATIONAL

BOOK YOUR SEATS IMMEDIATELY AND NO INCREASE
IN PRICES FOR THIS FABULOUS SHOW   **12/6   25/**

Obtainable from : Jack Solomons, 41 Gt. Windmill Street, W.1. Ger 9195/6. Wembley Stadium, Wembley 1234
Len Mancini, "Lord Palmerston", 648 King's Road, S.W.6. REN 4501. Jim Smith, 102 Ophir Road, Northend, Por
Jim Wicks, 139 Footscray Road, Eltham, S.E.9. Eltham 5254. Alex Griffiths, Deauville, Dingle Lane, Willenhall

M ✦ TUESDAY 18TH JUNE 1963

proudly presents

AND PERSONALITY ─ CASSIUS CLAY
"CASSIUS THE GREAT"

EIGHT CHAMPIONSHIP OF THE WORLD
E ROUNDS

JLOUS"

S CLAY

AVYWEIGHT CONTENDER
oung heavyweight. The world's greatest personality

ENERY"

OOPER

With the best straight left and left hook in the world

Cooper K.O.'s Dick Richardson

EATEST FIGHTER IN THE WORLD   I'M THE GREATEST POET IN THE WORLD
EATEST PREDICTOR IN THE WORLD   I'M THE NEXT CHAMPION OF THE WORLD

PORTING BOUTS FOR THIS NIGHT OF ALL NIGHTS

£2.2.0   £3.3.0   £4.4.0   and   £6.6.0

s A'Beckett, 320 Old Kent Road, S.E.1. ROD 7334. Alf Mancini, "Rifle", 80 Fulham Palace Road, W.6. RIV 6502.
3132.   H. Gorman, 9 Lynton Place, Rumney, Cardiff. Lew Phillips, 177 Corporation Street, Birmingham. CEN 3652.
nd usual Agents

AILLSONS (PRINTERS) LTD. LEICESTER PHONE 21212

By mid-1963, with 19 wins under his belt, 15 of which were knockouts, Clay had begun his ascension on the international boxing stage. These early fights were not without difficulty, however. In his fight against rival Sonny Banks at Madison Square Garden in New York, Clay was knocked down in the 4th round, only to return and prove victorious with a TKO. In Clay's first overseas professional bout, the undefeated boxer was pitted against British heavyweight champion Henry Cooper who was known for his trademark left hook. Clay's winning streak continued, downing Cooper after five rounds, but the match did not come without its fair share of controversy. Clay's trainer, Angelo Dundee was accused of stalling match time to fix a tear in Clay's right glove and calling for new gloves (which couldn't be immediately found) and defying match rules by administering smelling salts.

★ ★ ★ ★

DID YOU KNOW?

In these early days, Clay quickly became known for his braggadocio and outspoken attitude. In his professional foreign debut against the much-loved Henry Cooper, Clay's loud mouth and humiliation tactics during the fight didn't fare well with the British public. During the weigh-in, Clay is said to have proclaimed, "You got a Queen, you need a King. I am King!" It was this behavior that earned him the nickname "Louisville Lip".

"I figured that if I said it enough, I would convince the world that I really was the greatest."

★ ★ ★ ★

DID YOU KNOW?

In what has since become regarded as one of the most iconic meetings of the 20th century, Clay met with The Beatles during their first tour of the US in February 1964. After initially being declined a visit to Sonny Liston, the band dropped by on one of Clay's training sessions at the Fifth Street Gym in Miami, Florida on February 18. The British "mop tops" mugged for the cameras and clowned around with the young boxer, but not even they—who were making history on a daily basis—realized the enormity of the meeting. At the time, John Lennon referred to Clay as a "big-mouth who's going to lose".

In 1973, Lennon made amends somewhat by writing Ringo Starr a song called 'I am the Greatest' for his album *Ringo*.

On the night before the heavyweight title fight on February 24, 1964, Cassius Clay released the following poem to an insatiable media.

Clay comes out to meet Liston and Liston starts to retreat,
If Liston goes back an inch farther he'll end up in a ringside seat.
Clay swings with a left, Clay swings with a right,
Just look at young Cassius carry the fight.
Liston keeps backing but there's not enough room,
It's a matter of time until Clay lowers the boom.
Then Clay lands with a right, what a beautiful swing,
And the punch raised the bear clear out of the ring.
Liston still rising and the ref wears a frown,
But he can't start counting until Sonny comes down.
Now Liston disappears from view, the crowd is getting frantic
But our radar stations have picked him up somewhere over the Atlantic.
Who on Earth thought, when they came to the fight,
That they would witness the launching of a human satellite.
Hence the crowd did not dream, when they laid down their money,
That they would see a total eclipse of Sonny.

"Float like a butterfly, sting like a bee. The hands can't hit what the eyes can't see."

M20. v Sonny Liston (US)
Miami Beach, FL (United States) February 25, 1964
TKO 7 (15) Win: 20–0 Record (22 years, 39 days)

Won WBA, WBC, The Ring & Lineal Heavyweight titles.

In February 1964, Clay was poised to grab the WBA/
WBC heavyweight title from boxing powerhouse
"Big Bear" Sonny Liston. Despite his unblemished
record, Clay entered the ring as a seven-to-one
underdog. These odds did little to place a dent in
Clay's confidence, with the 22-year-old hurling insults
at title-holder Liston. In the build up to the bout,
Clay is quoted as calling Liston a "big, ugly bear". It
was also in the lead up to this fight that Clay uttered
the line "float like a butterfly, sting like a bee", which
would become one of the most memorable quotes
in sporting history. With his famous fancy footwork,
Clay shocked punters to take out Liston with a
technical KO in seven rounds. Clay was crowned world
heavyweight champion, declaring "I am the greatest"
in the wake of his win.

Following Clay's upset over Liston in the world
heavyweight championship, the boxers became
embroiled in controversy. A technicality, which
prevented Clay and Liston from signing on for a
rematch, would subsequently see Clay stripped of
his WBA/WBC title and Liston removed from the
WBA/WBC rankings.

LISTON

WORLD'S HEAVYWEIGHT CHAMPIONSHIP BOUT!!

CLAY

Tale of the Tape

LISTON		CLAY
215	Weight	215
6'1"	Height	6'2¹/₂"
84	Reach	79
44	Chest (norm)	42¹/₂
46¹/₂	Chest (exp.)	44¹/₂
33	Waist	34
25¹/₂	Thigh	25
15¹/₂	Fist	13
17¹/₂	Neck	17¹/₂
17¹/₂	Biceps	15
29	Age	22

On February 26, 1964, Clay confirmed that he had joined the Nation of Islam and had rejected his "slave name" Cassius Clay. On March 6, he adopted the "holy" name of Muhammad Ali. Later that year, on August 14, he married his first wife Sonji Roi.

Ali moved away from the Nation of Islam in the 1970s after it was discovered leader Elijah Muhammad fathered several children out of wedlock and was using the organization's funds to support up to 19 children born to various mothers. In the 1980s Ali converted to the Sunni Muslim sect.

At the time of Clay's conversion, the Nation of Islam was headed by Elijah Muhammad (1897–1975). Among the religion's most high profile recruits was former prisoner Malcolm Little, who took on the title Malcolm X. Among the sect's more militant views at the height of America's civil rights movement was the pursuit of racial separation and the establishment of a black religious state. When Malcolm X tried to break away from the Nation of Islam, he was assassinated by radical members of the group at a rally in February 1965.

"Cassius Clay is a slave name. I didn't choose it and I don't want it. I am Muhammad Ali, a free name. It means beloved of God—and I insist people use it when people speak to me and of me."

"I'm the king of the world, I am the greatest, I'm Muhammad Ali. I shook up the world. I am the greatest."

"I'm king of the world.
I'm pretty, I'm pretty.
I'm a baaaad man, you heard
me, I'm a baaad man.
Archie Moore fell in four,
Liston wanted me more,
so since he's so great,
I'm a make him fall in eight.
I'm a baaad man,
I'm king of the world!
I'm 22 years old and ain't
gotta mark on my face.
I'm pretty. I easily survived
six rounds with that
ugly bear, because
I am the greatest."

M21. v Sonny Liston (US)

Lewiston, ME (United States) May 25, 1964
KO 1 (15), Win: 21–0 Record (23 years, 128 days)

Retained WBC, The Ring & Lineal Heavyweight titles.

The second meeting between Ali and Liston was fraught with controversy, with most venues across the US reluctant to host the rematch due to strict WBA ruling. A fight was finally set for November 1964 at the Boston Garden in Massachusetts. Ali once again entered the match as an underdog, with the odds against him 13 to five, but approached the rematch with his usual antics, carrying a bear trap to pre-match physicals. Just three days out from the event, Ali was rushed to hospital for a strangulated hernia, thus delaying the bout for another six months. The highly anticipated event was postponed once again due to suspected links between the promoters and organized crime. The Boston venue was cancelled and after much scrambling, Ali and Liston took to the ring in Maine in May 1965.

In what became one of the most controversial fights in boxing history, Ali went on to defeat Liston in a first-round knockout with a "phantom punch" that still causes debate. Ali's victory was overshadowed by the violence and controversies surrounding the event, with the match setting the record for the lowest attendance at a heavyweight championship.

★ ★ ★ ★

DID YOU KNOW?

In the Ali v Liston fight, in which Ali was again the underdog with bookmakers, was one of the fastest title fights in history. Sonny Liston hit the canvas at 1:44, got up at 1:56, and referee Walcott stopped the fight at 2:12. Many thought Liston had "taken a dive".

"Get up and fight, sucker!" Ali screamed at Liston as he stood over him on the canvas. "Nobody will believe this!"

★ ★ ★ ★

"You don't have to be in a boxing ring to be a great fighter. As long as you are true to yourself, you will succeed in your fight for that in which you believe."

"I am America.
I am the part you
won't recognize.
But get used to me.
Black, confident, cocky;
my name, not yours;
my religion, not yours;
my goals, my own;
get used to me."

M22. v Floyd Patterson (US)

Las Vegas, NV (United States) November 22, 1965

TKO 12 (15), Win: 22–0 (Record) 23 years, 309 days

Retained WBC, The Ring & Lineal Heavyweight titles.

With the Ali–Liston saga over, Ali channeled his energy towards new rival Floyd Patterson, a former WBA title holder. Patterson, suffering a bruised ego after losses to Liston, came out of hiding to take on Ali in November 1965. Like most of Ali's fights, the opponents exchanged taunts in the build up to the match, with Patterson refusing to call Ali by his new name and calling him "a disgrace" to the sport and his nation. Patterson entered the match with a back injury which proved vital to Ali's victory after 12 rounds.

The crowd booed Ali for prolonging the beating for the last six rounds as punishment for Patterson's apparent disrespect. "Come on America!" Ali taunted Patterson as he continued to punch him. "Come on white America. What's my name? Is my name Clay? What's my name fool?"

"My trainer don't tell me nothing between rounds. I don't allow him to. I fight the fight. All I want to know is did I win the round. It's too late for advice."

★ ★ ★ ★

DID YOU KNOW?

Drew "Bundini" Brown (1928–1987) was a member of Muhammad Ali's training entourage who was responsible for writing much of the poetry the champ recited to publicize his bouts. A trainer recommended to the Angelo Dundee camp by former champion Sugar Ray Robinson, Bundini Brown was regarded as the "oxygen" to Ali's fire. "Cook, champ, cook!" he would shout from Ali's corner.

Brown also coined the phrase "float like a butterfly, sting like a bee" (which he copyrighted) and was a consummate showman in his own right. When Ali labeled Liston "The Bear", it was Bundini who brought the bear trap. A part-time actor (*Shaft*, 1970 and *The Color Purple*, 1985) and unsuccessful screenwriter, Brown was also responsible for the following tortured prose that Ali recited many times during his career.

I've wrestled with alligators / I've tussled with a whale / I done handcuffed lightning / And throw thunder in jail. / Only last week I murdered a rock / injured a stone / Hospitalized a brick / I'm so mean I make medicine sick.

★ ★ ★ ★

M23. v George Chuvalo (Canada)

Toronto (Canada) March 29, 1966
UD 15 (15) Win: 23–0 Record (24 years, 71 days)

Retained WBC, The Ring & Lineal Heavyweight titles.

M24. v Henry Cooper (UK)

London, (UK) May 21, 1966
TKO 6 (15), Win: 24–0 Record (24 years, 124 days)

Retained WBC, The Ring & Lineal Heavyweight titles.

M25. v Brian London (UK)

London, (UK) August 6, 1966
KO 3 (15) Win: 25–0 (24 years, 201 days)

Retained WBC, The Ring & Lineal Heavyweight titles.

M26. v Karl Mildenberger (W. Germany)

Frankfurt (W. Germany) September 10, 1966
TKO 12 (15), Win: 26–0 Record (24 years, 236 days)

Retained WBC, The Ring & Lineal Heavyweight titles.

"If you even dream of beating me you'd better wake up and apologize."

"My way of joking is to tell the truth. That's the funniest joke in the world."

In 1966, Ali's controversial personal life once again stole the spotlight. With the Vietnam War raging, Ali was drafted into the US Army but refused to serve on religious grounds. Amidst the controversy and media outcry, Ali travelled overseas to fight in matches in Canada and Europe, proving victorious in all matches. While scheduled to fight WBA champion Ernie Terrell in a bout in Toronto, Canada, last minute complications saw Ali take on George Chuvalo instead. Ali defeated substitute Chuvalo in the 15-round match.

In the UK, Ali continued his overseas winning streak, conquering Henry Cooper for a second time, and the aptly named British boxer Brian London. Ali then progressed to Germany, where he claimed victory in a 12-round battle against Karl Mildenberger.

"It's not bragging if you can back it up."

 ### M27. v Cleveland Williams (US)
Houston, TX (United States) November 14, 1966
TKO 3 (15), Win: 27–0 Record (24 years, 301 days)

Retained WBC, The Ring & Lineal Heavyweight titles.

 ### M28. v Ernie Terrell (US)
Houston, TX (United States) February 6, 1967
UD 15 (15) Win: 28–0 Record (25 years, 20 days)

Retained WBC, The Ring & Lineal Heavyweight titles.
Won WBA title.

 ### M29. v Zora Folley (US)
New York, NY (United States) March 22, 1967
KO 7 (15), Win: 29–0 Record (25 years, 64 days)

Retained WBC, WBA, The Ring & Lineal
Heavyweight titles.

"It's hard to be humble, when you're as great as I am."

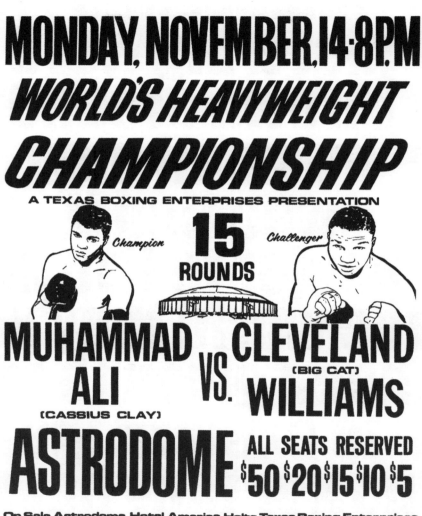

"Impossible is just a big word thrown around by small men who find it easier to live in the world they've been given than to explore the power they have to change it."

After his return from overseas championship fights, Ali took on Cleveland "Big Cat" Williams in late 1966. At a clear physical disadvantage from a prior shooting incident, Williams was downed by Ali in just three rounds at the Houston Astrodome in Texas. This performance remains a highlight of Ali's career.

In 1965 Canada's Ernie Terrell defeated Eddie Machen to win the vacant WBA championship. He defended the title twice before losing to Muhammad Ali in February 1967. Ali beat Terrell, his toughest opponent since Sonny Liston, in what is considered to be one of the ugliest fights in boxing history. Terrell held on for a brutal 15 rounds, before Ali was crowned the winner in a unanimous decision to unite the WBC and WBA & NYSAC world titles.

This win was followed by a seven-round knockout against US rival Zora Folley. On April 28, 1967 the WBA, WBC, the NYSAC and several other US state boxing commissions withdrew recognition of Muhammad Ali as champion for his refusal to be inducted into the United States Army.

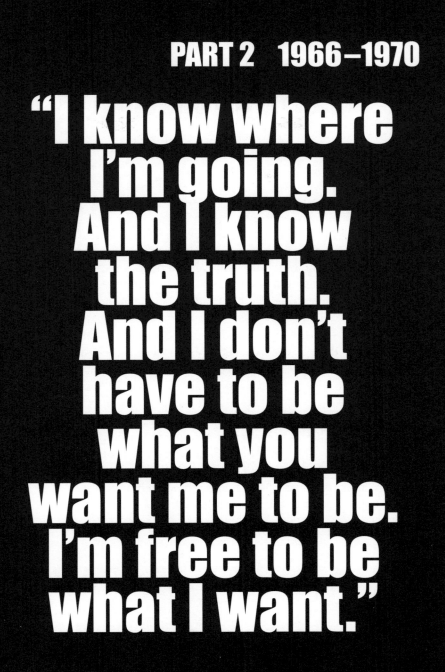

"I know where
I'm going.
And I know
the truth.
And I don't
have to be
what you
want me to be.
I'm free to be
what I want."

"I ain't got no quarrel with those Vietcong."

Ali was well known for his outspoken views on the Vietnam War and his refusal to be drafted for military service because of his religious views. He attended the induction ceremony in April 1967, but refused to step forward. His claim that, since he was a Muslim minister he was unable to fight in the war, was rejected. On April 29, 1967 he was stripped of his world titles, fined $10,000 and his boxing licence was suspended.

In June, Ali was found guilty of refusing induction into the US Army. Convicted by an all-white jury of draft evasion and sentenced to five years in prison, he appealed against the outcome. His passport was revoked.

On January 27, 1970, after a long legal battle, Ali's boxing license was restored. On July 28, the Supreme Court overturned Ali's 1967 conviction by unanimous verdict, ruling that Ali was not guilty of evading the military because he should not have been drafted in the first place due to his religious beliefs.

"My conscience won't let me go shoot my brother, or some darker people, or some poor hungry people in the mud for big powerful America. And shoot them for what? They never called me nigger, they never lynched me, they didn't put no dogs on me, they didn't rob me of my nationality, rape and kill my mother and father ... Shoot them for what? How can I shoot them poor people? Just take me to jail."

★ ★ ★ ★

DID YOU KNOW?

During his time in boxing exile, Ali continued his campaign against the Vietnam War, speaking at rallies and on college campuses. Ali's involvement in Islam also grew during this time and he soon became a prominent spokesperson in the US civil rights movement. To make ends meet, Ali turned his hand to musical theatre, starring in the Broadway musical *Buck White* in 1969.

As public opinion and the tide turned on the Vietnam War, so did support for Ali.

★ ★ ★ ★

"Why should they ask me to put on a uniform and go ten thousand miles from home and drop bombs and bullets on brown people in Vietnam while so-called Negro people in Louisville are treated like dogs and denied simple human rights? No, I am not going ten thousand miles from home to help murder and burn another poor nation simply to continue the domination of white slave masters of the darker people the world over. This is the day when such evils must come to an end.

I have been warned that to take such a stand would put my prestige in jeopardy and could cause me to lose millions of dollars which should accrue to me as the champion. But I have said it once and I will say it again. The real enemy of my people is right here. I will not disgrace my religion, my people or myself by becoming a tool to enslave those who are fighting for their own justice, freedom and equality ...

If I thought the war was going to bring freedom and equality to 22 million of my people, they wouldn't have to draft me, I'd join tomorrow. But I either have to obey the laws of the land or the laws of Allah. I have nothing to lose by standing up for my beliefs. So I'll go to jail. We've been in jail for four hundred years."

"If I ever was to get in the ring with Joe, here's what you might see:

Ali comes out to meet Frazier, but Frazier starts to retreat. If Joe back up an inch farther, he'll wind up in a ringside seat. Ali swings with his left. Ali swings with his right. Just look at the kid carry the fight. Frazier keeps backin', but there's not enough room. It's only a matter of time before Ali lowers the boom. Ali swings with his right. What a beautiful swing. But the punch lifts Frazier clean out of the ring. Frazier still rising, and the referee wears a frown 'cause he can't start countin' till Frazier comes down. Frazier's disappeared from view.

The crowd is getting frantic. But our radar stations done picked him up. He's somewhere's over the Atlantic. Now, who would've thought, when they came to the fight, they was gonna witness the launching of a black satellite?

But don't wait for that fight. It ain't never gonna happen.

The onliest thing you can do is wonder and imagine."

While Ali was suspended, another undefeated boxer usurped his heavyweight crown in the form of "Smokin' Joe" Frazier (1944–2011). Ali was often asked during this time what would happen if he ever got the chance to get back into the ring and fight Frazier. His reply was typically forthright (see left).

★ ★ ★ ★

DID YOU KNOW?

In 1969, a fictional "Super Fight" between Rocky Marciano (1923–1969) and Muhammad Ali was released. Two years before, when the only undefeated heavyweight champions were Ali and Rocky Marciano, producer Murray Woroner programmed all the available statistical information into a NCR 315 computer and received the following result—Marciano won in a split points decision.

Ali (suspended) and Marciano (retired) agreed to get into the ring and recreate some of the fictitious commentary generated by the computer—for a $10,000 fee, a cut of the documentary profits and without either boxer knowing the final decision. Marciano was killed in a plane crash before the results could be revealed.

★ ★ ★ ★

M30. v Jerry Quarry (US)
Atlanta, GA (United States) October 26, 1970
TKO 3 (15), Win: 30–0 Record (28 years, 282 days)

Retained The Ring & Lineal Heavyweight titles.

M31. v Oscar Bonavena (Argentina)
New York, NY (United States) December 7, 1970
TKO 15 (15), Win: 31–0 (28 years, 324 days)

Retained The Ring & Lineal Heavyweight titles.

After spending more than three years in exile, Ali returned to the ring in October of 1970 to defeat Jerry Quarry in a three-round victory in Atlanta, Georgia. In front of a sell-out crowd, this was Ali's first match since his victory over Folley in 1967. In December 1970, with his boxing licence now officially reinstated, Ali fought Argentinian Oscar Bonavena at Madison Square Garden, New York. After a tough 14 rounds, Ali downed Bonavena in the 15th to yet again claim victory.

After just two professional fights following a three-year layoff, Ali rushed into a title bout with the similarly unbeaten Joe Frazier in a bid to reclaim the championship that had been taken from him.

"I had to prove you could be a new kind of black man. I had to show the world."

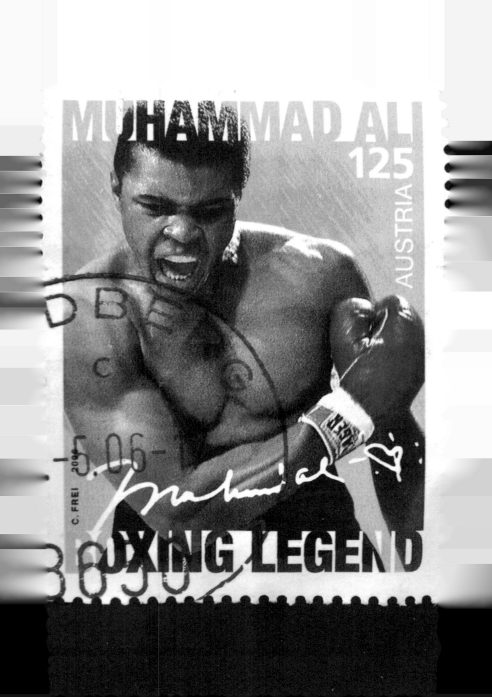

"The fight is won or lost far away from witnesses—behind the lines, in the gym, and out there on the road, long before I dance under those lights."

★ ★ ★ ★

DID YOU KNOW?

For the Ali v Quarry fight, Ali was yet to have his boxing licence fully reinstated. Aided by a State Senator, Ali was granted licence to fight in the state of Georgia, the only state without a boxing commission. Not long after, the federal courts ruled that Ali had been unjustly denied a licence, thus granting him permission to fight again across all US states.

★ ★ ★ ★

The Story of Two Champions

April 27, 1968 to February 16, 1970
Jimmy Ellis, WBA

Ellis defeated Jerry Quarry to win the vacant WBA championship, after an eight-man, three-round tournament to fill the title vacated by Ali's suspension. Ellis advanced to the championship match by defeating Oscar Bonavena in the semi-final and Leotis Martin in the first round. Quarry advanced by defeating Thad Spencer and former champion Floyd Patterson. Former WBA champion Ernie Terrell and Karl Mildenberger also participated in the tournament. Joe Frazier was invited to take part but declined.

★ ★ ★ ★

DID YOU KNOW?

In 1967, Ali joined Martin Luther King Jr. in the boxer's hometown of Louisville, where a bitter and violent struggle was being waged for fair housing. Ali spoke to the protesters saying: *In your struggle for freedom, justice and equality I am with you. I came to Louisville because I could not remain silent while my own people, many I grew up with, many I went to school with, many my blood relatives, were being beaten, stomped and kicked in the streets simply because they want freedom, and justice and equality in housing.*

★ ★ ★ ★

"Joe Frazier is so ugly that he should donate his face to the US Bureau of Wildlife."

March 4, 1968 to February 16, 1970
Joe Frazier, NYSAC

While Ali was suspended, Joe Frazier defeated Buster Mathis in a 1968 bout recognized by the athletic commissions of Illinois, Maine, Massachusetts, New York and Pennsylvania for the world championship title. Similar world championship recognition was given to him by the athletic commission of Texas after a victory over Dave Zyglewicz on April 22, 1969.

February 16, 1970 to January 22, 1973
Joe Frazier, Universal

On February 16, 1970 Joe Frazier and WBA champion Jimmy Ellis fought to unify the world heavyweight championship. Ellis was the recognized champion of the WBA and WBC, whose title had remained vacant following the suspension of Muhammad Ali in 1967. Joe Frazier was awarded the championship when he defeated Ellis on February 16, 1970. Frazier then defeated Ali on March 8, 1971 to claim the undisputed world title.

✊ M32. v Joe Frazier (US)

New York, NY (United States) March 8, 1971
UD 15 (15), Loss: 31–1 Record (29 years, 50 days)

For WBA & WBC World Heavyweight titles.
Lost The Ring & Lineal Heavyweight titles.

In March 1971, Ali took on reigning heavyweight champion Joe Frazier in what was billed as the "Battle of the Champions". The contest, which pitted two undefeated heavyweight champions against each other, was the most highly anticipated fight in boxing history. Ali held his ground against an overpowering Frazier for 14 rounds, but was ultimately knocked down in the 15th by a hard left hook. Frazier took out the championship in a unanimous victory, affording Ali his first public defeat in his entire boxing career. It is claimed Ali had been suffering the impact of "ring rust" after years spent away from the sport.

"I'll beat him so bad he'll need a shoehorn to put his hat on."

FIGHT PICTURES

BATTLE OF THE CHAMPIONS

IN COLOR

CASSIUS CLAY

JOE FRAZIER

VS.

MUHAMMAD ALI

JOE FRAZIER

WILL NOT BE SHOWN ON HOME TV FOR AT LEAST 6 MONTHS!

★ ★ ★ ★

DID YOU KNOW?

Up until his loss against Frazier, Ali remained undefeated for 31 professional fights. Ali's loss to Frazier fuelled ongoing animosity between the pair, which lasted until Frazier's death in 2011. Punches were even exchanged beyond the ring, as witnessed during a televised interview in which Frazier tackled Ali to the ground.

This match was the first time the boxing world witnessed the "rope-a-dope" strategy. This tactic involved Ali leaning against the ropes while he absorbed Frazier's punches, all in the hope of tiring his opponent. Ali's strategy would prove unsuccessful in this match, but he would refine and master the tactic and win back the world championship.

★ ★ ★ ★

M33. v Jimmy Ellis (US)

Houston, TX (United States) July 26, 1971
TKO 12 (12), Win: 32–1 Record (29 years, 190 days)

Won vacant NABF Heavyweight title.

M34. v Buster Mathis (US)

Houston, TX (United States) November 17, 1971
UD 12 (12), Win: 33–1 Record (29 years, 304 days)

Retained NABF Heavyweight title.

M35. v Jürgen Blin (W.Germany)

Zurich (Switzerland) December 26, 1971
KO 7 (12), Win: 34–1 Record (29 years, 343 days)

"Silence is golden when you can't think of a good answer."

BUGNER

TS ON SALE HERE

ALSO

RS PALACE AND

ENTION CENTER

S
52°

JIM NABORS

IN

DERBIRD LOUNGE
STCOTT TRIO
TAVISH & THE CLAN

T Bird Jewels

★ ★ ★ ★

DID YOU KNOW?

Former British Heavyweight Champion Joe Bugner trained with Ali as a sparring partner during 1970. At the time, Ali was on the comeback trail following his suspension from US boxing in the years prior. Ali and Bugner took to the ring on two occasions—in 1973 in Las Vegas, and a world title bout in Kuala Lumpur (Malaysia) in 1975. Ali was victorious in both matches but Bugner remains the only boxer to "go the distance" with Ali in two 15-round contests without being knocked out.

★ ★ ★ ★

"It's just a job. Grass grows, birds fly, waves pound the sand. I beat people up."

Eager to reclaim his winning reputation, Ali quickly bounced back from his loss to Frazier and took on a series of opponents in 1971–72 with the hope of building up to another title fight. Ali took to the ring once again against Jerry Quarry, defeating his opponent with a total knockout after seven rounds. He claimed victory in his second encounter with Floyd Patterson and downed Bob Foster to win all six fights in 1972.

M36. v Mac Foster (US)
Tokyo (Japan) April 1, 1972
UD 15 (15), Win: 35–1 Record (30 years, 75 days)

M37. v George Chuvalo (Canada)
Vancouver (Canada) May 1, 1972
UD 12 (12), Win: 36–1 Record (30 years, 105 days)

M38. v Jerry Quarry (US)
Las Vegas, NV (United States) June 27, 1972
TKO 7 (12), Win: 37–1 Record (30 years, 162 days)

M39. v Alvin Lewis (US)
Dublin (Republic of Ireland) July 19, 1972
TKO 11 (12), Win: 38–1 Record (30 years, 184 days)

M40. v Floyd Patterson (US)
New York, NY (United States) September 20, 1972
TKO 7 (12), Win: 39–1 Record (30 years, 247 days)

M41. v Bob Foster (US)
Stateline, NV (United States) November 21, 1972
KO 8 (12), Win: 40–1 Record (30 years, 309 days)

M42. Joe Bugner (UK)
Las Vegas, NV (United States) February 14, 1973
UD 12 (12), Win: 41–1 Record (31 years, 28 days)

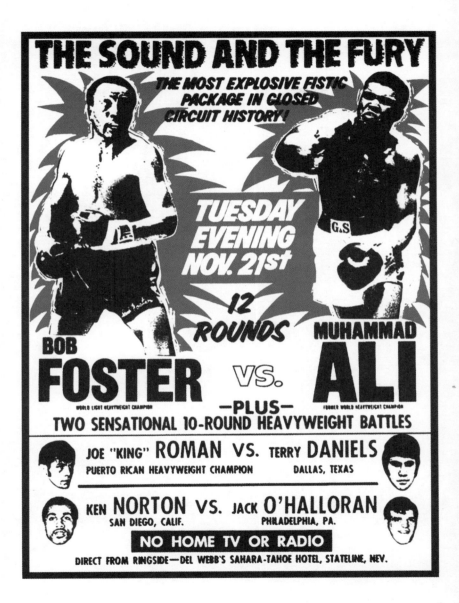

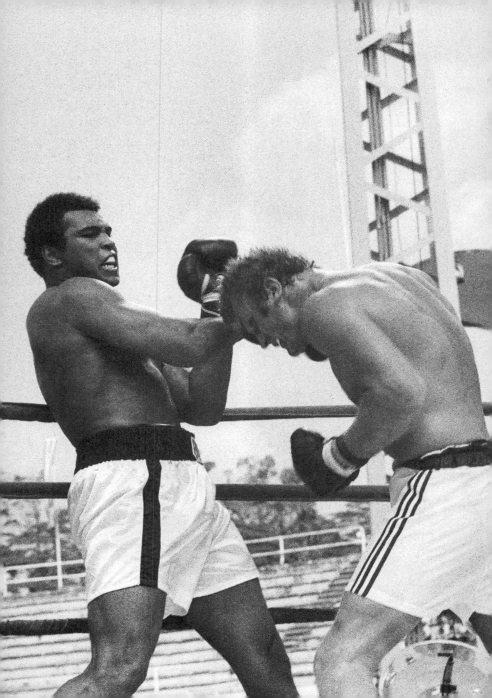

"Don't count the days; make the days count."

M43. v Ken Norton (US)
San Diego, CA (United States) March 31, 1973
SD 12 (12) Loss: 41–2 Record (31 years, 73 days)

Lost NABF Heavyweight title.

M44. v Ken Norton US)
Inglewood, CA (United States) September 10, 1973
SD 12 (12) Win: 42–2 Record (31 years, 236 days)

Won NABF Heavyweight title.

M45. v Rudie Lubbers (NED)
Jakarta (Indonesia) October 20, 1973
UD 12 Win: 43–2 Record (31 years, 276 days)

"I never thought of losing, but now that it's happened, the only thing is to do it right. That's my obligation to all the people who believe in me. We all have to take defeats in life."

In 1973, Ali suffered his second career loss in the match against Ken Norton in San Diego, California. The contest finished after Norton had landed a punch in round 10 that broke Ali's jaw, and Ali lost a unanimous points decision. This defeat resulted in Ali immediately seeking a second bout only six months later. Ali also changed his training routine for this fight, shedding the huge entourage that Angelo Dundee had built around him and training at a secluded camp away from the media attention he enjoyed so much. Back to peak form, Ali took down Norton in the controversial 12-round match. Shortly after the fight, Ali is quoted as stating "Ken Norton is the best man I have ever fought". A month after the fight, Ali took on Dutchman Rudi Lubbers in Jakarta, Indonesia to bag victory in 12 rounds.

★ ★ ★ ★

DID YOU KNOW?

Former Dutch heavyweight champion Rudi Lubbers' life post-boxing was marred by crime and alcohol addiction. Following a four-year stint in prison for drug trafficking, the once successful sportsman worked at carnivals and funfairs before becoming homeless.

★ ★ ★ ★

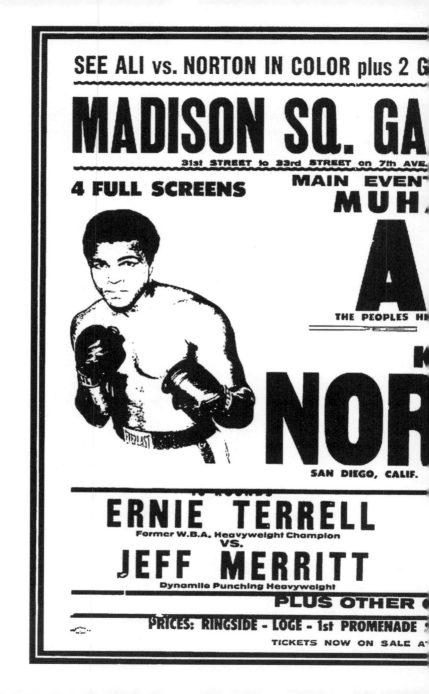

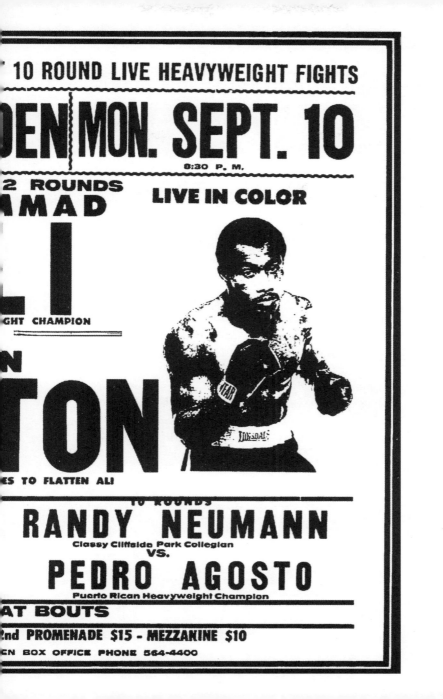

♟ M46. v Joe Frazier (US)
New York, NY (United States) January 28, 1974
UD 12 (12) Win: 44–2 Record (32 years, 11 days)

Retained NABF Heavyweight title, vacated later in 1974.

In January 1974, after recovering from the lost ground
in his earlier defeat to Frazier, Ali donned his gloves
for a non-title rematch against old rival Joe Frazier.
The boxers met for a second time at Madison Square
Garden, New York for what is considered to be
the least exciting match in the Ali v Frazier trilogy.
Keen to avenge his loss to Frazier three years before,
Ali entered the fight a 7/5 favorite. Throughout
the 12 rounds, Frazier's notorious left hook yet
again proved troubling for Ali. Despite complaints
of holding too much during the fight, Ali went on
to claim the North American Boxing Federation
heavyweight title in a unanimous points decision.

With this victory, Ali had shown he was ready for
another crack at the world heavyweight title which was
then held by the imposing George Foreman.

"To be the greatest. You must believe you are the best. If you're not, pretend you are."

FIGHT II...THE BIG FIGHT EV

MADISON SQ. GAI

31st ST. TO 33rd STREET ON 7th AVE.

MAIN EVENT

J

FRA

PHILA. — FORMER WOR
1964 OLY

MUHA

A

LOUISVILLE, KY. — FORMER
1960 OLY

OTHER GREAT HE

PRICES $100 RINGSIDE AND LOC

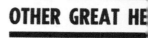

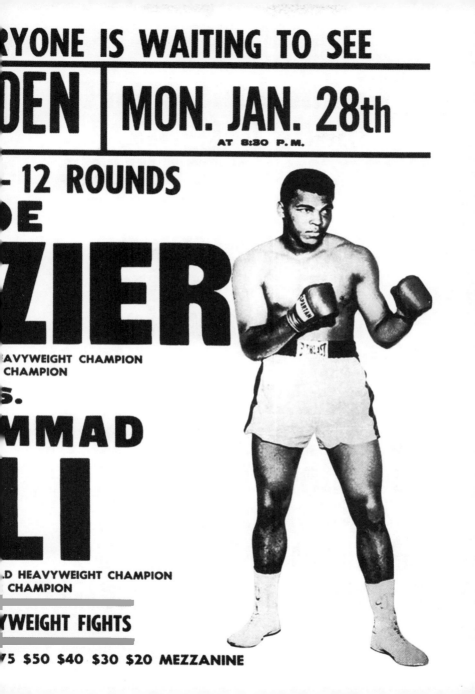

"Champions aren't made in gyms. Champions are made from something they have deep inside them—a desire, a dream, a vision. They have to have last-minute stamina, they have to be a little faster, they have to have the skill and the will. But the will must be stronger than the skill."

DID YOU KNOW?

The battle for the North American Boxing Federation heavyweight title was the second of three highly significant encounters between Ali and Frazier. Both the first and third encounters were named "Fight of the Year" by influential boxing magazine *The Ring*. Although considered the least exciting of the three fights, the second meeting was far from insignificant. Ali and Frazier were both keen to avenge past losses, with each hoping to secure a shot at the world heavyweight title.

★ ★ ★ ★

"We can't be brave without fear."

M47. v George Foreman (US)
Kinshasa (Zaire) October 20, 1974
KO 8 (15), Win: 45–2 Record (32 years, 286 days)

Won WBC, WBA, The Ring & Lineal Heavyweight titles.

Ali's victory against Frazier paved the way for a second
shot at the world heavyweight title in Kinshasa,
Zaire (now the Democratic Republic of the Congo)
in October 1974. Ali took on 25-year-old world
heavyweight champion George Foreman in a legendary
match billed as "The Rumble in the Jungle". Ali set
about the fight in a rare underdog position, with
analysts dismissing the 32-year-old in favor of the
younger Foreman. In a massive upset, Ali silenced
critics, knocking out Foreman in just eight rounds
to become the second boxer in history to regain the
world heavyweight championship. This fight has
since become the most famous in boxing history and
showcased Ali's brilliance utilizing the "rope-a-dope"
technique.

"If you were surprised when Nixon resigned, just watch what happens when I whup Foreman's behind!"

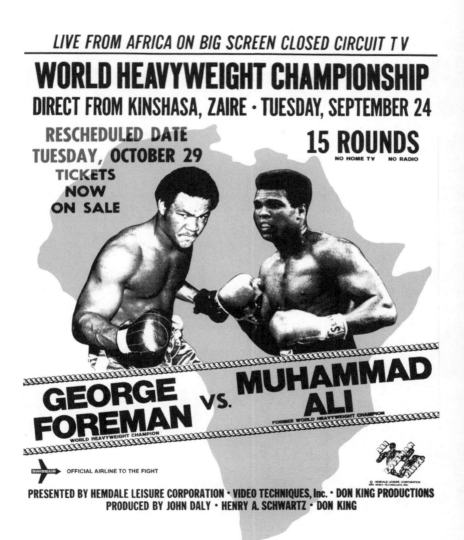

LIVE FROM AFRICA ON BIG SCREEN CLOSED CIRCUIT T V

WORLD HEAVYWEIGHT CHAMPIONSHIP

DIRECT FROM KINSHASA, ZAIRE · TUESDAY, SEPTEMBER 24

RESCHEDULED DATE
TUESDAY, OCTOBER 29
TICKETS
NOW
ON SALE

15 ROUNDS
NO HOME TV   NO RADIO

GEORGE
FOREMAN
WORLD HEAVYWEIGHT CHAMPION

VS.

MUHAMMAD
ALI
FORMER WORLD HEAVYWEIGHT CHAMPION

SWISSAIR   OFFICIAL AIRLINE TO THE FIGHT

© HEMDALE LEISURE CORPORATION
1974 VIDEO TECHNIQUES, INC.

PRESENTED BY HEMDALE LEISURE CORPORATION · VIDEO TECHNIQUES, Inc. · DON KING PRODUCTIONS
PRODUCED BY JOHN DALY · HENRY A. SCHWARTZ · DON KING

"No one starts out on top. You have to work your way up. Some mountains are higher than others, some roads steeper than the next. There are hardships and setbacks, but you can't let them stop you. Even on the steepest road, you must not turn back. You must keep going up. In order to reach the top of the mountain, you have to climb every rock."

Zaire, a poor, developing nation now known as the Democratic Republic of the Congo, was selected as the fight location as the nation's president, Mobuto Sese Seko, was keen for the publicity the event would bring to the country. Ali was supportive of this selection and the economic boost it would provide for the nation. The fight was scheduled for 4 am, in order to accommodate US audiences and was televised in 100 countries around the world. The crowd chanted "Ali boma ye!" which loosely means "Ali kill him!".

★ ★ ★ ★

DID YOU KNOW?

Ali's victory was the inspiration for British singer Johnny Wakelin's hit "Black Superman (Muhammad Ali)" in early 1975. The song was No.1 in Australia, Top 10 in the UK and Top 40 in the US, although Ali later distanced himself from the song (he received none of the profits). Wakelin's follow up song "In Zaire", also about the Foreman v Ali fight, was not as successful.

★ ★ ★ ★

M48. v Chuck Wepner (US)
Richfield, OH (United States) March 24, 1975
TKO 15 (15), Win: 46–2 Record (33 years, 66 days)

M49. v Ron Lyle (US)
Las Vegas, NV (United States) May 16, 1975
TKO 11 (15) Win: 47–2 Record (33 years, 119 days)

Retained WBC, WBA, The Ring & Lineal
Heavyweight titles.

In 1975, Ali chose moderately performed journeyman
Chuck Wepner as his first title defense in 1975. The
Ali v Wepner battle saw the reigning heavyweight
champion knocked down in the 9th round, only to
rise to victory with a TKO in the 15th round. After
the fight, eager to save face, Ali claimed his 9th round
knockdown was due to tripping on Wepner's foot.

It was Wepner's never-give-up attitude which later
inspired Hollywood star Sylvester Stallone to write the
Oscar-winning film *Rocky* with nemeses Apollo Creed
loosely based on Ali.

"Allah is the Greatest.
I'm only the greatest boxer."

"For the black man to come out superior would be against America's teachings. I have been so great in boxing they had to create an image like Rocky, a white image on the screen, to counteract my image in the ring. America has to have its white images, no matter where it gets them. Jesus, Wonder Woman, Tarzan and Rocky."

The story
you only
think
you know!

Ernest Borgnine   Annazette Chase   Robert Duvall   James Earl Jones   Lloyd Haynes   David Huddleston   Ben Johnson   John Marley   Dina Merrill   Roger E Mosley   Mira Waters   Paul Winfield

THE GREATEST

Columbia Pictures Presents MUHAMMAD ALI in "THE GREATEST"

★ ★ ★ ★

DID YOU KNOW?

At the 1977 Academy Awards, Ali surprised actor Sylvester Stallone onstage and jokingly accused him of "stealing my story" for his Oscar-nominated film *Rocky* (1976) and the pair shaped up as if to fight. Ali brought his own story to the screen later that year, with the film adaptation of his best-selling autobiography *The Greatest*. Ali, who had some acting experience, played himself (who else) as did "Bundini" Brown, while Academy Award winning actor Ernest Borgnine took on the role as trainer Angelo Dundee. The film was not a commercial success (director Tom Gries died of a heart attack before the film was released), but Ali later appeared as a former slave in the TV movie *Freedom Road* (1979) with Kris Kristofferson.

Ali (while still known by his former name, Clay), actually made his Hollywood debut in the 1962 film *Blood Money*, knocking out Anthony Quinn. He later remarked, "When I saw the movie, I felt so sorry for him."

★ ★ ★ ★

M50. v Joe Bugner (UK)
Kuala Lumpur (Malaysia) June 30, 1975
UD 15 (15), Win: 48–2 record (33 years, 164 days)

Retained WBC, WBA, The Ring & Lineal
Heavyweight titles.

★ ★ ★ ★

DID YOU KNOW?

Ali took on Joe Bugner, for a second time in their respective careers, in Kuala Lumpar in June 1975 to acclimatize for the fight against Joe Frazier in Manila later that year. Malaysia is a strict Muslim country and Ali received death threats because he had been a celebrity judge at a beauty contest and kissed the winner when presenting the trophy. Joe Bugner received death threats because he was a white Christian taking on a black Muslim hero. No wonder the boxing ring was full of armed soldiers before the contest.

★ ★ ★ ★

MUHAMMAD ALI
vs JOE BUGNER

Stadium Merdeka, Kuala Lumpur, Malaysia. 1st. July 75

"I'm not the greatest, I'm the double greatest. Not only do I knock 'em out, I pick the round. I'm the boldest, the prettiest, the most superior, most scientific, most skilfullest fighter in the ring today."

★ ★ ★ ★

DID YOU KNOW?

Ali was famous for predicting what round he would end a fight, with varying success, but trainer Angelo Dundee was also known to slip a piece of paper into Ali's gloves with the predicted round the bout would end written on it. In the fight against Richard Dunn in 1976, Ali wrote "KO" and "Round 5" on the inside of his gloves before the fight so they could be immediately auctioned for charity. Dunn was stopped in round 5.

Of course, Ali wasn't always correct in his predictions. He famously said that he would knock out Sonny Liston in the 6th round of their 1965 rematch. He did it in the first!

★ ★ ★ ★

M51. v Joe Frazier (US)
Quezon City (Philippines) October 1, 1975
TKO 14 (15), Win: 49–2 Record (33 years, 257 days)

Retained WBC, WBA, The Ring & Lineal
Heavyweight titles.

The much-acclaimed third bout between boxing
legends Ali and Frazier took place in October 1975
in Manila, the Philippines. Billed as "The Thrilla in
Manila", the fight took place in extreme conditions
(temperatures reached almost 100°F /37.8°C) and saw
both boxers endure extreme punishment. In the later
rounds, Ali used his rope-a-dope tactic to conquer an
ailing, swollen-eyed Frazier, who failed to answer the
bell for the 15th round. The match proved testing for
Ali, with him noticeably physically spent and slumping
on his stool at the end of the contest.

"It will be a killer, and a chiller, and a thriller, when I get the gorilla in Manila"

"I always bring out the best in men I fight, but Joe Frazier, I'll tell the world right now, brings out the best in me. I'm gonna tell ya, that's one helluva man, and God bless him."

★ ★ ★ ★

DID YOU KNOW?

Alongside the first Ali v Frazier encounter, "The Thrilla in Manila" is considered one of the most famous boxing battles of all time. Ali later stated that the match was the closest he has ever felt to dying. Both fighters took heavy punishment, but Frazier's corner refused to let him come out for the 15th and final round just when Ali's corner was considering the same option.

Ali also had another fight on his hands in Manila. Ali was joined by his girlfriend Veronica, who was mistakingly introduced to Philippine President Ferdinand Marcos as Ali's wife. This was seen on US TV by Ali's wife Belinda, who hurriedly flew to the Philippines to confront the boxer. The pair was soon divorced and Veronica became Ali's third wife in 1977.

★ ★ ★ ★

M52. v Jean-Pierre Coopman (BEL)
San Juan (Puerto Rico) February 20, 1976
KO 5 (15), Win 50–2 (34 years, 34 days)

M53. v Jimmy Young (US)
Landover, MD (United States) April 30, 1976
UD 15 (15), Win 51–2 (34 years, 104 days)

M54. v Richard Dunn (UK)
Munich (W.Germany) May 24, 1976
TKO 5 (15), Win 52–2 record (34 years, 128 days)

M55. v Ken Norton (US)
The Bronx, NY (United States) September 28, 1976
UD 15 (15), Win 53–2 Record (34 years, 255 days)

M56. v Alfredo Evangelista (URG)
Landover, MD (United States) May 16, 1977
UD 15 (15), Win 54–2 Record (35 years, 119 days)

M57. v Earnie Shavers (US)
New York, NY (United States) September 29, 1977
UD 15 (15), Win 55–2 Record (35 years, 255 days)

Retained WBC, WBA, The Ring & Lineal
Heavyweight titles.

During the period 1976–77, Ali's career fights included three with Jean-Pierre Coopman, Jimmy Young and Richard Dunn. He won all three. In September 1976, Ali and Ken Norton met for a third time in what has since been deemed one of the most disputed title fight decisions in history. Ali ultimately won the highly-contested match in 15 rounds, after which he announced his retirement to practice his faith. This decision would be premature, with Ali returning in May 1977 to defeat Alfredo Evangelista in 15 rounds in Landover, Maryland.

At 35 years of age, Ali took on Earnie Shavers in New York in a display that showed the champion was beyond his prime. Albeit a struggle for Ali, the legendary boxer came out on top, winning in the 15th round. Following the match, fears for Ali's health caused his long-time doctor to recommend he hang up his gloves.

"If my mind can conceive it, and my heart can believe it —then I can achieve it."

Muhammad Ali v Antonio Inoki

On June 26, 1976, Ali embarked on what has since become a forgotten bout of his career against Japanese wrestler Antonio Inoki. The mixed boxing/wrestling match took place in Tokyo, Japan and was the first time a boxer and martial artist had contested the ring.

As an unusual case, special rules were predetermined for the match, with debates lingering to this day as to whether the match was actually scripted. In an attempt to shape the match into an entertaining spectacle, it was originally arranged for Ali to accidently knock out the referee, and, in these moments of confusion, receive a knockout blow at the hands of Inoki. The match itself however, resulted in a 15-round draw, leaving many to continue to debate the legitimacy of the result.

★ ★ ★ ★

DID YOU KNOW?

This Inoki fight is regarded as one of the most embarrassing matches of Ali's career. Actor-writer-director Sylvester Stallone even used it for inspiration in *Rocky III* (1982) when he had his character Rocky Balboa take on wrestler Thunderlips (played by Hulk Hogan).

★ ★ ★ ★

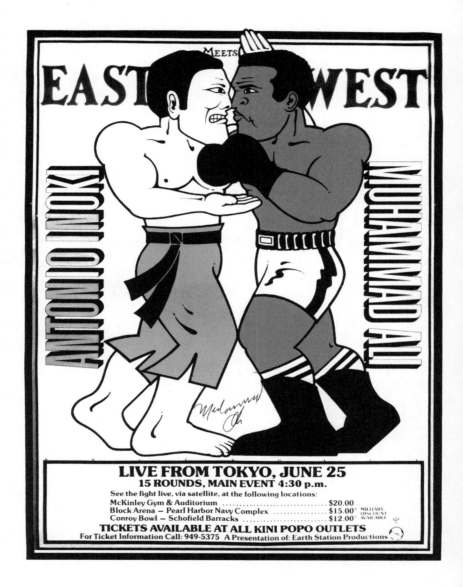

"**Impossible** is just a big word thrown around by small men who find it easier to live in the world they've been given than to explore the power they have to change it."

"Impossible is not a fact. It's an opinion. Impossible is not a declaration. It's a dare. Impossible is potential. Impossible is temporary. Impossible is nothing."

M58. v Leon Spinks (US)

Las Vegas, NV (United States) February 15, 1978
SD 15 (15), Loss 55–3 (36 years, 29 days)

Lost WBC, WBA, The Ring & Lineal Heavyweight titles.

Despite suggestions from his former doctor Ferdie Pacheco to consider retiring from the sport, Ali continued to fight. In February 1978, Ali entered the ring at the Hilton Hotel in Las Vegas against Leon Spinks, a far less experienced boxer who began the match as a 10–1 underdog. Ali's performance during the 15-round match was far from the highlight of his career, resulting in a loss by split decision. Ali was clearly out of shape during the match.

Leon Spinks (born 1953) was no stranger to glory in his shock win over Ali in their first match-up in 1978. In 1976, he won gold in the light-heavyweight division of the Montreal Olympic Games. Spinks then won the world heavyweight title in his eighth professional fight, the most inexperienced champion in history.

★ ★ ★ ★

DID YOU KNOW?

After winning the title in March, Leon Spinks agreed to a rematch with Muhammad Ali. For the first time in history, a sanctioning organization (WBC) withdrew its recognition of a world champion because of Spinks' refusal to fight its designated mandatory challenger, Ken Norton. At the time, Norton had been designated the WBC's mandatory challenger based on a victory over Jimmy Young.

For the first time in the Heavyweight division, Ken Norton was immediately recognized as the WBC champion when Leon Spinks signed a contract for a rematch with former champion Muhammad Ali on March 18, 1978. Upon being named champion, Norton was required to defend the title against the organization's new mandatory challenger, Larry Holmes. Norton lost that bout on June 9, 1978, bringing his reign as champ to an end.

★ ★ ★ ★

M59. v Leon Spinks (US)
New Orleans, LA (United States) September 15, 1978
UD 15 (15), Win 56–3 (36 years, 241 days)

Won WBA, The Ring & Lineal Heavyweight titles.

Following Ali's loss to Spinks earlier in the year, the boxers went head to head again in September of 1978 in another shot at the heavyweight title. Spinks' reign as champion proved brief and a sharper, fitter Ali went on to reclaim the title in a 15-round unanimous decision to become the first heavyweight boxer to win the championship three times. The match at the New Orleans Superdome broke attendance records with the largest indoor attendance ever at a boxing match.

"Only a man who knows what it is like to be defeated can reach down to the bottom of his soul and come up with the extra ounce of power it takes to win when the match is even."

"There are no pleasures in a fight, but some of my fights have been a pleasure to win."

★ ★ ★ ★

DID YOU KNOW?

Ali's success against Leon Spinks in 1978 saw him become the first three-time world heavyweight champion. Announcing his retirement on April 27, 1979, Ali relinquished his WBA title in exchange for a payment from promoter Don King, who was trying to stage a bout between WBC champion Larry Holmes and John Tate for the undisputed world crown. The bout never happened, but Tate defeated Gerrie Coetzee on October 20, 1979 to win the vacant WBA title. Ali would return to the ring in 1980 and lose to Holmes.

★ ★ ★ ★

"I'm retiring because there are more pleasant things to do than beat up people."

Ali's response when asked to make up a poem about himself.
It was later reported that Ali meant the more childlike 'Me, Whee!'
but we prefer the more inclusive poem originally reported.

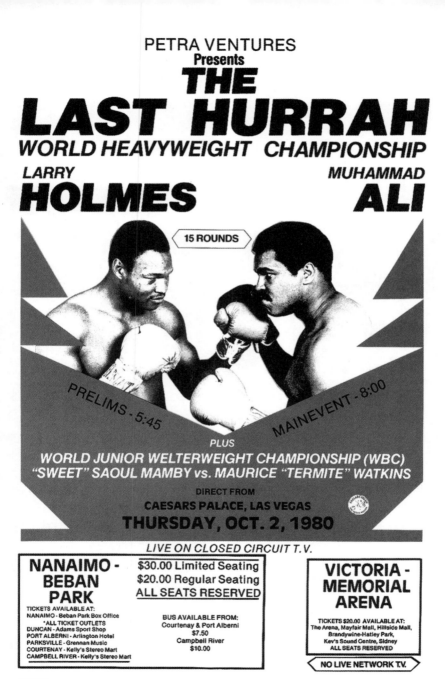

M60. v Larry Holmes (US)
Las Vegas, NV (United States) October 2, 1980
TKO 10 (15) Loss: 56–4 Record (38 years, 259 days)

Lost The Ring & Lineal Heavyweight titles.

A little more than a year after his retirement from boxing, Ali announced that he would fight current Heavyweight Champion Larry Holmes in Las Vegas in October 1980. His comeback, which was prompted by financial reasons, afforded Ali a crack at a fourth world heavyweight title win. Ali's return to boxing was short-lived, however, and he was defeated by a younger Holmes in a technical knockout in 11 rounds. Holmes had dominated the match, landing 125 punches in the final rounds alone, and Ali's trainer, Angelo Dundee, stopped the fight at the end of the 10th round.
It was Ali's only loss without "going the distance" for a judges' decision. Ali blamed the loss on thyroid medication he took prior to the fight, but 20 years after his professional boxing debut, he was a shadow of his former champion self.

"I am an ordinary man who worked hard to develop the talent I was given. I believed in myself, and I believe in the goodness of others."

"I hated every minute of it. But I said to myself, 'Suffer now, and live the rest of your life as a champion'."

★ ★ ★ ★

DID YOU KNOW?

Larry Holmes (born 1949) became heavyweight champion on June 9, 1978 when he defeated Ken Norton. He later relinquished his WBC title in order to assume the championship of the International Boxing Federation (IBF), a newly formed organization which had splintered off from the WBA. Holmes defeated his old sparring partner Ali in 1980 and remained undefeated champion until December 11, 1983 when he was beaten by underdog Michael Spinks—the younger brother of Leon Spinks—just one win shy of matching Rocky Marciano's all-time record win record of 49–0.

Holmes too would come out of retirement in 1988 but was knocked out by champion Mike Tyson in the 4th round. Holmes would continue boxing until 2002 but never won another title.

★ ★ ★ ★

✊ M61. v Trevor Berbick (Canada)

Nassau (The Bahamas) December 11, 1981
UD 10 (10) Loss: 56–5 Record (39 years, 328 days)

In one last hurrah, Ali took on Trevor Berbick in a fight in The Bahamas in December 1981. Promoted as the "Drama in Bahama", Ali signed up for the fight following his loss to Larry Holmes in the WBC heavyweight title match the previous year. With growing concerns for Ali's ailing health, the boxer persevered with the fight and was subsequently beaten after 10 rounds in a unanimous decision. Although Ali put on a tough fight for the first seven rounds, his age and health would eventually stand in the way of victory. Following the loss, Ali announced his retirement from the sport, boasting a career record of 56 wins to five losses over a 21-year career.

Struggling with the early stages of Parkinson's disease, Ali's continued boxing is believed to have contributed further to his condition, which affected him throughout much of his later life.

★ ★ ★ ★

DID YOU KNOW?

Trevor Berbick, the man who earned the tag of being "the last man to fight Muhammad Ali" was murdered in Jamaica in 2006 at the age of 52.

★ ★ ★ ★

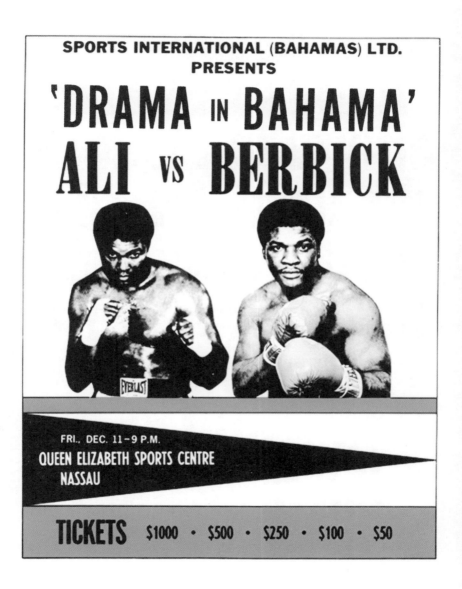

"A rooster crows only when it sees the light. Put him in the dark and he'll never crow. I have seen the light and I'm crowing."

★ ★ ★ ★

DID YOU KNOW?

Ali's trainer Angelo Dundee (1921–2012) was in the champ's corner for all but two of his professional fights: the first against Tunny Hunsaker in 1960, and the fight against Jimmy Ellis in 1971. Ellis was also Dundee's boxer, and a sparring partner of Ali's, and Dundee decided Ellis needed him more. During his career, Dundee also worked with 15 other world boxing champions including Sugar Ray Leonard, José Nápoles, George Foreman, George Scott, Jimmy Ellis, Carmen Basilio, Luis Manuel Rodríguez and Willie Pastrano.

Ironically, Dundee was in Trevor Berbick's comer when the heavyweight champion was destroyed by 20-year-old challenger Mike Tyson in two rounds in November 1986. In 2005, Dundee trained actor Russell Crowe to fight like a depression-era fighter for the film *Cinderella Man*, the story of world champion James J. Braddock.

★ ★ ★ ★

"Service to others is the rent you pay for your room here on earth."

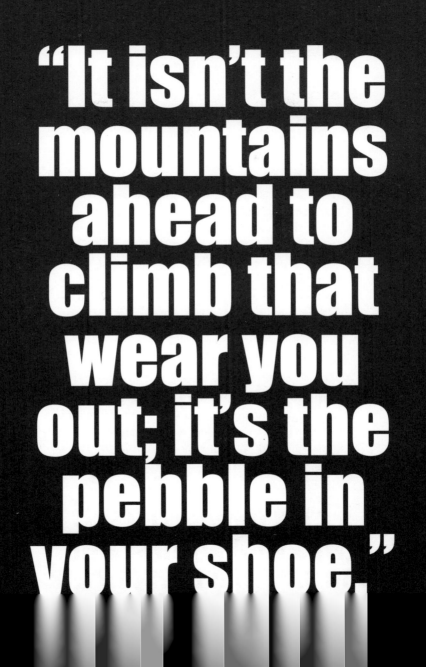

"It isn't the mountains ahead to climb that wear you out; it's the pebble in your shoe."

Marriages & Children

Spouses: Sonji Roi (m. 1964, div. 1966)
Belinda Boyd (m. 1967, div. 1977)
Veronica Porché Ali (m. 1977, div. 1986)
Yolanda Williams (m. 1986–2016)

Muhammad Ali was married four times. His first marriage, at the young age of 22 in 1964, was to Sonji Roi, a cocktail waitress. After less than 18 months of marriage, the pair divorced in January 1966. Shortly afterwards, Ali met and married Belinda Boyd in 1967. This marriage produced four children: Maryum (born 1968), twins Jamillah and Rasheda (born 1970) and Muhammad Ali Jr (born 1972). During this time, Ali also fathered two daughters, Miya (born 1972) and Khaliah (born 1979) in extramarital relationships. In 1977, Boyd and Ali's marriage ended when details of his affair with model and actress Veronica Porche were made public. Two daughters, Hana (1976) and Laila Ali (1977), were born during his marriage to Veronica. Ali's fourth marriage was in 1986 to Yolanda Williams. They adopted a son, Asaad Amin and remained married up until Ali's death in June 2016.

"My toughest fight was with my first wife, and she won every round."

"At home I am a nice guy: but I don't want the world to know. Humble people, I've found, don't get very far."

"Inside of a ring or out, ain't nothing wrong with going down. It's staying down that's wrong."

"Parkinson's is my toughest fight. No, it doesn't hurt. It's hard to explain. I'm being tested to see if I'll keep praying, to see if I'll keep my faith. All great people are tested by God."

"A man who views the world the same at 50 as he did at 20 has wasted 30 years of his life."

Muhammad Ali was diagnosed with the progressive neurological condition Parkinson's disease in 1984. He was 42. The average age of diagnosis is 65 years, however younger people can also be diagnosed with Parkinson's (Young Onset Parkinson's). Symptoms of Parkinson's develop slowly and gradually progress over time. While there is no known cause for Parkinson's, the onset of symptoms is directly related to a decline in the production of the brain chemical, dopamine. A lack of dopamine often results in people having difficulty controlling their movements and moving freely.

Because Ali was only in his early forties when diagnosed, many believe that prolonged punishment to his head—especially in his later years—may have contributed to the onset of the condition. Not all boxers contract Parkinson's disease, defenders of the sport rightly argue, but most boxers do suffer side effects from repeated head trauma including slurred speech, memory loss and even dementia.

1996: Atlanta Olympics

At the 1996 Summer Olympics in Atlanta, when the moment came to ignite the cauldron to signal the start of the Games, Muhammad Ali stepped forward from the dark to hold up the Olympic flame. His body was shaking noticeably, especially his arm holding the torch, but he brought his ailing body under enough control to complete the task. It was one of the most spine-tingling moments in Olympic Games history.

Later, during the Atlanta Games, he was given a second gold medal to replace the one he tossed in Ohio River 36 years earlier.

★ ★ ★ ★

DID YOU KNOW?

Leon Gast's 1996 documentary *When We Were Kings*, won the Oscar for Best Documentary Feature at the 1997 Academy Awards. The film was shot in 1974 but took decades to complete because the negatives and rights were caught up in civil suits involving the Liberians who originally financed it. The film is now regarded as one of the best sports documentaries ever made.

★ ★ ★ ★

"The man who has no imagination has no wings."

Muhammad Ali and Joe DiMaggio
wearing gold medals, Ellis Island,
NY, January 1998.

★ ★ ★ ★

DID YOU KNOW?

Ali had an interesting, almost symbiotic relationship with boxing commentator Howard Cosell (1918–1995) over the years. Cosell was one of the first to interview the young champion after he defeated Liston in Miami in 1964, and the pair continued to spar verbally over the ensuing years.

The pair were complete opposites. One was a handsome athlete at the prime of his career and the other, a small balding lawyer turned broadcaster. Ali was black and Muslim, Cosell white and Jewish. However, boxing's "odd couple" shared the same ego-driven ability to self-promote and entertain.

The pair were also kindred spirits. When Ali was suspended for avoiding the draft in 1967, Cosell actively campaigned to allow him to earn a living while appealing his conviction. They remained friends, antagonists and media co-conspirators until Cosell's retirement in the early 1990s, before lung cancer claimed him.

★ ★ ★ ★

In 1997 Ali received the Arthur Ashe Courage Award—a sport-oriented award not limited to sports-related people or actions—presented annually to individuals whose contributions transcend sports. The award, presented by ESPY (Excellence in Sports Performance Yearly Awards), honors the memory of tennis legend Arthur Ashe (1943–1993) who waged a public fight against HIV-Aids. Ashe was diagnosed with HIV after a blood transfusion during open-heart surgery.

Ironically, Howard Cosell won the award two years before Ali.

★ ★ ★ ★

DID YOU KNOW?

Ali, the movie starring Will Smith as the man himself, was released in 2001. It tells Ali's story between 1964 and 1974 covering his triumphant wins in the boxing ring as well as the controversies of becoming a Muslim, railing against the Vietnam War and his subsequent suspension from fighting.

Will Smith and fellow actor, Jon Voight were nominated for Best Actor and Best Supporting Actor at the Oscars. The movie was nominated for 25 film awards of which it won 10.

Smith was one of the pallbearers for Ali's memorial service.

★ ★ ★ ★

"What you
are thinking
you are
becoming."

"All through my life, I have been tested. My will has been tested, my courage has been tested, my strength has been tested. Now my patience and endurance are being tested."

★ ★ ★ ★

DID YOU KNOW?

In 1997, Muhammad Ali was named "Sportsman of the Century" by *Sports Illustrated*, beating such people as Babe Ruth (baseball), Jesse Owens (athletics) and Mark Spitz (swimming). The Ali (then Clay) versus Liston fight in 1964 was voted No. 4 in the top 10 sporting moments of the 20th century.

In 1999, the British public named him BBC Sports Personality of the Century.

★ ★ ★ ★

"Ever since I first came here in 1963 to fight Henry Cooper, I have loved the people of England ... They have always been extremely warm and welcoming to me, which is why I am especially honored to accept the BBC's Sports Personality of the Century. I give thanks to God and to all the people in the UK who have supported me over the years."

In 2005, Muhammad Ali was awarded the Presidential Medal of Freedom, the highest US civilian honor, by the then President George W. Bush.

In 2012, he was awarded the Liberty Medal in Philadelphia, for his long time activism in humanitarian causes, civil rights and religious freedom.

★ ★ ★ ★

DID YOU KNOW?

In 1980, Muhammad Ali offered to travel to Iran to mediate in the freedom of 60 US embassy personnel who were being held hostage after the fall of Iran and the overthrow of the Shah by Islamic fundamentalists. The revolutionists rejected Ali's offer when the US government said it would not hand over the Shah, who had fled to the US with his family.

A decade later, however, he traveled to Baghdad, Iraq, and secured the release of 15 US contractors after dictator Saddam Hussein invaded Kuwait and was holding them hostage. Ali successfully gained the hostages' release in November 1990 before the US bombed Iraq and turned the course of the Gulf War.

★ ★ ★ ★

"Hating people because of their color is wrong. And it doesn't matter which color does the hating. It's just plain wrong."

★ ★ ★ ★

DID YOU KNOW?

On July 28, 2012, Ali joined a number of dignitaries and other special guests in escorting the Olympic flag during the 2012 Summer Olympic Games in Stratford, East London.

★ ★ ★ ★

"I am a Muslim and there is nothing Islamic about killing innocent people in Paris, San Bernardino, or anywhere else in the world... True Muslims know that the ruthless violence of so called Islamic Jihadists goes against the very tenets of our religion... We as Muslims have to stand up to those who use Islam to advance their own personal agenda... They have alienated many from learning about Islam. True Muslims know or should know that it goes against our religion to try and force Islam on anybody."

★ ★ ★ ★

DID YOU KNOW?

Ali left the public stage in recent years but continued to provide support to the Muhammad Ali Parkinson Center at Barrow Neurological Institutes, as well as other charities. On 9 April 2016, Ali made his last known public appearance at the Parkinson's fundraiser Muhammad Ali's Celebrity Fight Night XXII.

★ ★ ★ ★

Muhammad Ali died on June 3, 2016 as the result of septic shock due to unspecified natural causes. He was 74 years old.

The three-time heavyweight champion was buried in his hometown of Louisville, Kentucky on 10 June 2016. Ali planned his own funeral, which featured eulogies from former US President Bill Clinton, sportscaster Bryant Gumbel and comedian and close friend Billy Crystal who said, in part: "Ali forced us to take a look at ourselves."

President Barack Obama pays tribute

Muhammad Ali was The Greatest. Period.
If you just asked him, he'd tell you. He'd tell you
he was the double greatest; that he'd "handcuffed
lightning, thrown thunder into jail."

But what made The Champ the greatest—what truly
separated him from everyone else—is that everyone else
would tell you pretty much the same thing.

Like everyone else on the planet, Michelle and I
mourn his passing. But we're also grateful to God for
how fortunate we are to have known him, if just for a
while; for how fortunate we all are that The Greatest
chose to grace our time.

In my private study, just off the Oval Office, I keep
a pair of his gloves on display, just under that iconic
photograph of him—the young champ, just 22 years old,
roaring like a lion over a fallen Sonny Liston. I was too
young when it was taken to understand who he was—
still Cassius Clay, already an Olympic Gold Medal
winner, yet to set out on a spiritual journey that would
lead him to his Muslim faith, exile him at the peak of
his power, and set the stage for his return to greatness
with a name as familiar to the downtrodden in the
slums of Southeast Asia and the villages of Africa as it
was to cheering crowds in Madison Square Garden.

"I am America," he once declared. "I am the
part you won't recognize. But get used to me—black,
confident, cocky; my name, not yours; my religion,
not yours; my goals, my own. Get used to me."

That's the Ali I came to know as I came of age—not just as skilled a poet on the mic as he was a fighter in the ring, but a man who fought for what was right. A man who fought for us. He stood with King and Mandela; stood up when it was hard; spoke out when others wouldn't. His fight outside the ring would cost him his title and his public standing. It would earn him enemies on the left and the right, make him reviled, and nearly send him to jail. But Ali stood his ground. And his victory helped us get used to the America we recognize today.

He wasn't perfect, of course. For all his magic in the ring, he could be careless with his words, and full of contradictions as his faith evolved. But his wonderful, infectious, even innocent spirit ultimately won him more fans than foes—maybe because in him, we hoped to see something of ourselves. Later, as his physical powers ebbed, he became an even more powerful force for peace and reconciliation around the world. We saw a man who said he was so mean he'd make medicine sick reveal a soft spot, visiting children with illness and disability around the world, telling them they too could become the greatest. We watched a hero light a torch, and fight his greatest fight of all on the world stage once again; a battle against the disease that ravaged his body, but couldn't take the spark from his eyes.

Muhammad Ali shook up the world. And the world is better for it. We are all better for it. Michelle and I send our deepest condolences to his family, and we pray that the greatest fighter of them all finally rests in peace.

Response to George Plimpton's question at the end of an interview: "What would you like people to think about you when you've gone?"

"I'd like for them to say he took a few cups of love, he took one tablespoon of patience, teaspoon of generosity, one pint of kindness. He took one quart of laughter, one pinch of concern, and then, he mixed willingness with happiness, he added lots of faith, and he stirred it up well, then he spread it over his span of a lifetime, and he served it to each and every deserving person he met."

MGM
EPICALLY EXTRAORDINARY
CIRQUE DU SOLEIL
Muhammad Ali was Champion among Champions.
Like his talents and presence, his contributions to boxing were without peer.
Each time a fighter enters our ring

First published in 2016 by New Holland Publishers Pty Ltd
London • Sydney • Auckland

The Chandlery Unit 704 50 Westminster Bridge Road London SE1 7QY
United Kingdom
1/66 Gibbes Street Chatswood NSW 2067 Australia
5/39 Woodside Ave Northcote, Auckland 0627 New Zealand

www.newhollandpublishers.com

A record of this book is held at the British Library and the National
Library of Australia.

ISBN 9781742579184

Managing Director: Fiona Schultz
Publisher: Alan Whiticker
Design: Andrew Davies
Cover Design: Andrew Quinlan
Researcher: Kate Lockley
Project Editor: Susie Stevens
Production Director: James Mills-Hicks
Printer: Hang tai Printing Company
10 9 8 7 6 5 4 3 2 1

Keep up with New Holland Publishers on Facebook
www.facebook.com/NewHollandPublishers

US $12.99
UK £4.99